CU00919991

Faith for Children

Learning about God in the family

Christine Pedotti

Illustrations by Éric Puybaret

CTS Children's Books

Dear parents,

You are hoping to journey with your children in their discovery of the Faith, to awaken in them a sense of God's presence, and start them off on their lives as Christians. Soon they will be old enough to go to catechism classes, but you know that they will also need you and your witness. Perhaps, like many of us, you feel rather helpless. Perhaps you have forgotten what you learnt in catechism classes, and what you do remember seems too difficult for young children.

This little book is here to help. It is an introduction to the happiness and joy of getting to know God. It is an introduction to what it means to be baptised. Page by page, we will discover that we are Christians, that we belong to Christ. We will get to know Jesus, the Christ, who reveals his Father's love to us. He gives us his life and his Holy Spirit, and tells us that our lives are precious, because God loves us and invites us to a life of brotherly love; a life of happiness for ever.

Dear parents, I hope that this little book will help you to pass on all the richness of the Catholic faith, the Good News that we have received, so that our children will realise joyfully how good and how 'new' it is.

Christine Pedotti

Contents

Being baptised, I am a Christian

In baptism, the priest pours water onto the head of the person being baptised. The water of baptism is a sign of our entry into a new family, the family of Jesus' brothers and sisters, the family of God's children.

They are given a lighted candle because their whole life is lit up by baptism.

When people are baptised they are dressed all in white, all shining and new, to begin their new life.

Their godmother and godfather promise to help the newly baptised person to grow in this new life.

You can be be baptised at any age.
Parents usually have their children baptised when they are babies, but people can also be baptised when they are older, and even when they are grown up.

Lord, by baptism I become your child. You love me, you want me to grow and you want me to be happy.

I baptise you in the name of the Father,
and of the Son, and of the Holy Spirit. Amen.

Making the Sign of the Cross,

The Sign of the Cross wraps us in the love of God. In the name of the Father, we are much-loved children. In the name of the Son, we love each other as brothers and sisters. In the name of the Holy Spirit, we proclaim that love to the whole world.

I make the Sign of the Cross when I begin to pray.

I make the Sign of the Cross when I go into a church and at the beginning of Mass.

When someone is baptised, the parents, godfather, and godmother trace a cross on the person's forehead with their thumb, to welcome him or her into the great family of Christians. When we make the Sign of the Cross, we get ready to listen and celebrate with other Christians.

the sign of Christians

Lord, I turn to you, with my mind's intelligence, my heart's capacity for loving, and the strength of my shoulders.

Make a good Sign of the Cross. First touch your forehead, then your heart, then your shoulders, moving across from one to the other, left to right.

Christians are

We are Christians: that's our family name. Jesus Christ is the Son of God, and with him, we belong to God's family.

All men,

all women, and

are invited to belong to

"Christian" is a beautiful name. It comes from "Christ", which is another name for Jesus. He is often called Jesus Christ, or Christ Jesus.

the family of Jesus

*L*ord, take care of the whole of the Christian family, and make it grow even bigger.

all children on earth

the Christian family.

Jesus is the person God promised us

In the Bible, God made a great promise. He promised to send someone to help us know him better. This person would be chosen by God – as the Christ, the Messiah. In the land of Jesus, people prayed to God and waited for the person God had promised.

The prophets were God's spokesmen. They kept reminding everyone about the promise God had made.

Find all the extraordinary adventures of God's people in a Children's Bible, and ask your parents to read them or tell you about them. For Christians, the Bible is rather like a family album.

The Bible is a very big book that tells lots of stories about the friendship between God and his people. Sometimes the men and women in the Bible found it hard to understand God, and sometimes they did not like what God was asking of them, but God never abandoned them.

Jesus, you are
the Messiah
that God
promised us.

John the Baptist recognised Jesus:
he was the person promised by God.

Getting to Know the

The people in Jesus' country loved their land very much, because it was the land God had promised them, and he had kept his promise.

It was a beautiful country. Sometimes it got very hot, so the water in the wells and in the streams was precious.

About 2000 years ago, Jesus' country was occupied by the Romans.

Jesus lived in his family's village, **Nazareth**.

land of Jesus

Lord,
the fruits of the earth are
food for all the men, women
and children in the world.
Please teach us to share
them properly.

The earth was fertile, and people grew wheat to make bread, vines so they could eat the grapes and make wine, and olive-trees for oil.

The trees produced delicious, sweet fruit – dates, figs, and pomegranates.

Jerusalem was the capital city. It was a beautiful city built at the top of a hill. Jews came from all over the country to pray to God in the temple there. Jesus' country still exists today. It is called **Israel** or the **Holy Land**.

His mother is called Mary

Mary was a young girl from the little village called Nazareth. She was soon going to marry Joseph the carpenter, but something special happened to her.

The angel Gabriel asked Mary to be the mother of a child, who was to be the person God had promised. Mary said "Yes. I am the handmaid of the Lord."

An angel is a messenger from God.

In drawings and paintings, angels are shown with wings, because they come from God, as if flying down from Heaven.

The angel's visit to Mary is called the "Annunciation".

Hail, Mary,
full of grace,
the Lord is with thee.
Blessed art thou among women,
and blessed is the fruit of
thy womb, Jesus.

Joseph agreed to be father to this child who came from God,
and to look after him and his mother.

At Christmas, Christians

Christmas is a great feast-day, with lots of happiness and presents. The best Christmas present of all is Jesus. At Christmas we discover that God is with us. He came to live in our world, to make his home with us, and show that he loves us.

Today a saviour has been born to you.

The Roman Emperor wanted to count all the inhabitants of his Empire. Mary and Joseph set off for Bethlehem, the village where Joseph's family came from. It was there that the baby came into the world, in the middle of the night,

18

celebrate Jesus' birth

Glory to God
in the highest
and peace on earth
to those whom he loves.

He is Christ the Lord.

nice and warm in a stable, because there was no room left anywhere else. The angels in the sky sang about the good news, and **the shepherds from nearby came to adore the Baby Jesus.**

Getting to Know

Jesus' friends wrote down what they had seen and heard him do, in the books called the Gospels. The word "Gospel" means "good news". In the Gospels we can find out what Jesus did, what he said, and how he talked about God his Father.

There are four Gospels. They have the names of four of Jesus' friends: Matthew, Mark, Luke and John.

At Mass, the priest always reads a text from **the Gospel**. Everyone stands up to show that they are going to pay great attention.

Jesus

Lord, open my ears
and my heart so
that I can hear
and understand
the Good News.

"The Gospel of Jesus Christ
according to Saint John."

Jesus helps us to get

It is difficult to get to know God because we can't see him with our eyes, or hear him with our ears, or touch him with our hands. Luckily for us, God sent his Son Jesus to us. Jesus talks to us about God. He teaches us to speak to God as our very loving Father, saying "Our Father" to him.

Jesus' friends wanted to learn to pray just like him.

Jesus read the Bible too.

Sometimes we listen to our parents telling us about God, and sometimes we meet other Christians who believe in God. All of these believers are there to help us discover God in our turn. And throughout our lives we can hear the Word of God by reading or listening to the Bible.

to know God

Our Father,
who art in Heaven,
hallowed be thy Name.
Thy Kingdom come.
Thy Will be done on earth
as it is in Heaven.
Give us this day
our daily bread
and forgive us
our trespasses
as we forgive those who
trespass against us,
and lead us not
into temptation
but deliver us from evil.
Amen.

Believing in God, the creator

We believe that God is the creator. The world, with everything that lives in it, exists because he wanted it to. We believe men and women exist because God wanted them to live on the earth and learn to love each other.

God created man in his own image,

Loving means being like God, being the image of God.

of **heaven** and **earth**

Lord,
you have shared
a wonderful secret with us:
to find happiness,
all we need to do is
love each other.

nan and woman

he created them.

Believing God wants

God wants us to get to know him and be his friends. You want to grow and be happy - you're afraid of bad things and unhappiness. Well, God agrees with you. God is always on the side of happiness. He knows that there are sometimes bad things in our hearts (sin), but he promises us that the bad things won't win.

God gave Moses a Law (the Ten Commandments) so that the Israelites could live in happiness.

You can ask your parents to read you the story of Moses in a Children's Bible.

The Israelites spent forty years in the desert learning about God before reaching the land God had promised them.

us to be happy

*L*ord,
I believe that
you want us
to be happy.

Long ago, God
freed the Israelites,
who had been slaves
in Egypt. He parted the
sea, and everyone crossed
safely without even getting
their feet wet !

Jesus teaches us how to lead a good life

One day, Jesus began to talk about God to the people who lived in his country. The first words he spoke were words of happiness. Jesus was a happy person, because he knew what was good, and he did it. He taught us to love people and forgive them, and he showed us how.

Jesus forgave a woman who had abandoned her husband.

With Jesus, we can love people who don't love us, and even people who want to hurt us.

The first things Jesus said about happiness are called **the Beatitudes.**

Lord, I am still a child, but I want my life to be beautiful and good. Please show me the way.

Jesus tells us

Jesus talked about the happiness that was coming, the happiness of God who will rule over the whole world. He said: "The Kingdom of God is like a tiny seed. When it goes into the ground, it becomes a great tree, and everyone can shelter under it."

God gives married people the happiness of loving each other for their whole lives.

The birth of a new baby brings great happiness to the whole family!

You can give happiness to others too!

The happiness that is coming is called the Kingdom of God.

It is a Kingdom of love and happiness. Jesus promises it to us, and he tells us it is already here.

about happiness

Lord, teach me
to be happy
and to spread
happiness and
joy to those
around me.

Jesus calls some friends

Jesus called some friends to help him to tell the people in his country about God and about happiness. Today the job is not finished. Jesus invites us to be his friends and to announce to the whole world the happiness that comes from God.

Jesus doesn't just call special people. Lots of his friends were just fishermen who worked at the lakeside.

Jesus was also friends with two sisters, Martha and Mary, and their brother Lazarus.

The twelve apostles that Jesus chose to be with him were called Peter, Andrew, James, John, Philip, Bartholomew, Thomas, Matthew, another James, Jude, Simon and Judas. Peter was their leader.

Lord Jesus,
I want to be your
friend all my life.

Life is more

Jesus announced good news from God. God doesn't want us to be unhappy. He calls us to live a life that is beautiful and happy. At the wedding at Cana he turned water into wine so that the joy and celebrations weren't brought to an end.

The blind man Bartimaeus received his sight.

A paralysed man got up and started to walk.

Jesus brought Jairus's little daughter back to life.

Jesus cured people who were ill or unhappy.

By working all these miracles, Jesus showed that God loves us and that we really matter to him.

beautiful with Jesus

Lord, you don't like suffering or unhappiness. Give me a joyful heart and bring happiness to my family.

All his life, Jesus showed us that the most important thing of all, the thing that makes us happy, is to love truly. Jesus loves us so much that he gave his life for us.

On the last evening that he spent with his friends, Jesus shared a meal with them.
He took the bread and said: "This is my Body."
He took the wine and said: "This is my Blood."
"I give my life for love of you and of everyone."

Catholics remember this meal especially on Holy Thursday.
They repeat what Jesus said and did at Mass every Sunday.

the Last Supper

*L*ord, you give us your life and
you offer us an extraordinary
gift: the power of loving like you.
Thank you, Lord!

"In future, when you do as I have done, when you
eat this bread and drink this wine, it is my life,
the life of God, that you will receive."

Jesus gives his life:

Jesus had some enemies who did not believe that what he said was from God. They decided to put him to death to keep him quiet, and Jesus let them do it. Jesus never judged anyone, but they judged him. He never condemned anyone, but they condemned him. He gave love, and he received hatred. He never did anything wrong, but people did wrong to him. He died, nailed to a cross, but still forgave the people who killed him.

Jesus is arrested.

Jesus is condemned.

Christians remember Jesus' death on **Good Friday**

he **dies** on the **Cross**

Jesus dies on the cross.

Lord, sometimes I take part in doing wrong and hurting others. Please forgive me.

Jesus is laid in the tomb.

Jesus gives his life: he rises from the dead

Evil and hatred did not triumph over Jesus in the end. He did not stay in the tomb as death's prisoner. He is God, and he rose from the dead. He rose, and now he lives for ever. Jesus promises us that this good news is for us too. Our new life begins at Baptism. We have the promise that we will also be raised from the dead with Jesus, to live with him and with God his Father.

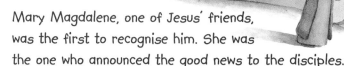

Mary Magdalene, one of Jesus' friends, was the first to recognise him. She was the one who announced the good news to the disciples.

Then Jesus appeared to the disciples. They really saw him, and spoke with him. Jesus was not dead any more, he had risen and is alive for ever!

The Resurrection is a completely new life, a life given by God for always, a life when we will never die again. This is the joy we celebrate at the great feast of Easter, singing "Alleluia! Alleluia!"

Lord Jesus,
I believe that you
are alive for ever.
I believe that I will
also be alive with you.
Alleluia!

41

Jesus sends the Holy

The risen Jesus left us and went back to his Father. He said that he was going to prepare a place for us. But he hasn't left us on our own: he has given us the Spirit of God, the Holy Spirit.

Jesus went back to his Father on the feast of the Ascension.

Jesus' friends received the Holy Spirit on the day of **Pentecost**. The Spirit gave them the courage to speak out. They weren't afraid of anything any more. They went to the ends of the earth to proclaim that Jesus had risen.

Spirit to his friends

Come, Holy Spirit,
give me strong faith
to believe in Jesus
the Risen One.
Give me courage
to proclaim it!

On the
day of
Pentecost,
Jesus' friends
proclaimed: "Yes,
Jesus is the one God
promised to send us. He
died on the cross and God
raised him from the dead.
We have seen him!"

With the Holy Spirit,

The Holy Spirit, whom you received when you were baptised, is your Defender. The Holy Spirit makes you stronger so that you can grow and learn to live like Jesus.

The Holy Spirit doesn't make you stronger to fight other people, he makes you stronger to love them and forgive them if they hurt you, just as Jesus did.

When Jesus talks about the Holy Spirit, he gives him rather a strange name: **the Paraclete** or **Defender**. The Holy Spirit is our Defender. He defends us against sin, fear and sadness.

I can **live** like **Jesus**

Holy Spirit,
please make us live
like brothers and sisters,
united in love.

The Holy Spirit helps me to do what is good.
The Holy Spirit is the Spirit of Jesus acting in me,
and he makes me live like a real son or daughter of God.

$\mathcal{L}$earning to do

When people are growing up, just like you, they need to learn to do what is right. The grown-ups around you, in your family and at school, can help you to understand and make the right choices.

The Spirit of God
to choose what is right even

Sometimes we refuse to listen, and we do unkind and naughty things on purpose. That is called sin.

We shouldn't confuse mistakes with sins. For example, if someone is clumsy and breaks a glass because he or she

what is right

I become truly free
when I am able to
choose what is right.
Thank you, Lord!

gives me the courage
when it's difficult to do.

wasn't being careful, that's an accident. But if someone
breaks something on purpose because he or she is in a temper,
that temper and bad action are a sin.

Loving, listening,

You are a Christian, and you have decided to live like Jesus and do what is right. Well done! That's the real way to happiness. How are you going to behave? Open your eyes, your ears, and your heart. Look at Jesus and listen to him.

Helping your parents...

Forgiving someone who has hurt you...

Love
one another

It's very simple to love, and it's the beginning of happiness for us and the people we love.

If we aren't brave enough, we can pray to the Holy Spirit to make us stronger.

sharing like Jesus

Lord Jesus,
give me the strength to love
people as you do, every day.

Sharing a game with your friends...

Celebrating with your family...

as I have loved you.

The forgiveness that gives life

Living and loving like Jesus isn't always easy. Even if you're still small, you know that sometimes you do things you're not supposed to, things that are naughty, silly or dangerous. Afterwards you feel as if nobody loves you or trusts you any more. But God forgives you and doesn't condemn you. When you say sorry and ask him to forgive you, he forgives you and forgets everything, because his love is bigger than your sins.

When you have said mean things, when you have hit your friend, or your brother or your sister, or when you have refused to obey your parents or teachers, you feel sad and upset.

To begin to love again, you have to say sorry.

We can say sorry to our parents and our friends. We can also say sorry to God for all the bad things we have in our hearts, even if nobody can see them.

God forgives us, and he gives us the strength not to do the same bad things again.

Lord,
sometimes my heart
is full of bad things.
I'm sorry.
Please forgive me,
and make my heart
happy again.

51

Learning to pray

When you pray, you can talk to God just like talking to a friend. You can pray at any time in the day – in the morning when you wake up, on the way to school, when you're enjoying being with your family, and when you're playing with your friends. You can pray alone in your bedroom, saying the words inside your head, or by saying a prayer out loud. You can also pray with others. The greatest prayer of Catholics is the Mass.

Good morning, Lord. Please help me to be good today.

Every day I am learning new things. I am growing in your love. Thank you, Lord!

Lord, please look after my family and everyone I love.

We can pray sitting down, because it makes us feel peaceful and calm. We can pray kneeling down, because everyone is very little before God. We can pray standing up, to show that we're ready to get going. We can shut our eyes, to think

I've had a great time with my friends and I'm really happy! Thank you, Lord!

It's the end of the day. I've tried to do what is right, but sometimes I've done wrong. I'm sorry, Lord. Give me the courage to do better tomorrow.

about God, or look around us and pray to God for the people we love. We can put our hands together to beg God for help, or open our arms wide to offer him our lives. There are lots of ways of praying. What matters is to trust in God.

The Church is the

You are a Christian, and your local church is your home too. It's often very big because it is the home of a very big family, the family of all Christians. The Church is also the name of the huge family of Christians throughout the world. Jesus is the head of the family. He invites everyone to come and join his family.

When you go into a church, keep quiet and pray. You are one of Christ's guests.

In the centre, there is a big table, called the altar. Jesus invites his family to share a special meal together.

If you go into church for Mass, the priest welcomes you in the name of Jesus Christ.

The **Tabernacle** is like a little chest. At the end of Mass, the priest places the Sacred Hosts in it – the bread which has become the Body of Jesus. A little light shines beside it. When we pass in front of the Tabernacle, we go down on one knee (genuflect), because Jesus is there.

home of Christians

Lord,
in your Church
you gather the
whole family of
Christians, and
you invite each
of us to join you.
Thank you, Lord!
Here I am!

55

On Sunday, Christians

Sunday is a special day. You don't have to go to school and your parents don't usually go to work. It's a special day for God, a feast day. On Sundays, Catholics go to Mass, the Lord's Supper. When we share that meal, we receive Jesus' life and we become like Jesus. We all sing together to show our joy.

We listen to readings from the Bible, the Word of God.

We share the bread and wine that have become the Body and Blood of Jesus. He gives us all his life and all his love.

The meal of the Mass has an unusual name: 'Eucharist', which means 'Saying thank-you'. We thank God for loving us, we thank him for Jesus, who is stronger than evil and unhappiness.

celebrate the Lord's day

Lord, you give us your life. You make us able to love each other as you love us yourself.

You have to be older to receive Holy Communion, but you can already say thank-you to God with all your heart.

The Spirit of Jesus

You become holy when you grow in God's love and let his Spirit guide you and teach you how to love more and more. Your first name may be one that belonged to a saint. Now that saint is living with God, and you can ask him or her to pray for you. He or she is your "Patron Saint".

Holy is the Lord!

On the Feast of All Saints, we celebrate all the saints who are living with God. In a way, this celebration is also about us, because God wants to share his life with us, and every day we can become holy like him.

makes us a holy people

Dear Patron Saint, you live with God.
Please watch over me so that
I may become holy,
and, together with all God's saints,
please pray for us.

Yes, the Lord God is holy.
He is good, just, full of love and tenderness,
and always ready to forgive us and welcome us.

Believing in the

You don't like thinking about death; it sounds frightening. That's normal, because we all prefer to think about life and happiness. God doesn't like death or fear or suffering either. He sent Jesus to make us a special promise: life and happiness will win in the end. Jesus was not kept prisoner by death, and people who have died will also rise again and will live in happiness with God.

When someone dies we are very sad, and everyone who knows them cries, because it's painful to be separated from people we love.

When someone has died, their body is placed in a wooden box called a coffin and buried in the ground in a cemetery.

We say that the dead are in Heaven, meaning that they are alive with God.

God of the living

*L*ord, I believe that you are the God of the living and that your friends who have died in this world are living in Heaven, in your love.

We can go to the cemetery and pray for people who have died.

Life is stronger

You are beginning to grow older, and you can see that sometimes terrible things happen in the world. There are wars, bad people, and disasters. God tells us: "Don't be afraid, I'm on your side. I am fighting against evil and unhappiness with you. And in the end, life and happiness will win!" But we have to realise that God won't do everything by himself; he wants you and wants everyone to join in. So let's get to work !

Peace
will be stronger than *war*.
Love
will be stronger than *hatred*.

There are people who don't know God, and they don't know that God loves them and wants them to be happy. That's very sad, and that's why we must tell everyone that God is our friend. **This is good news for everyone.**

than death

Lord,
I trust in you.
I believe that you are
always on our side.
Thank you!

Joy will be stronger than sadness.

CTS Children's Books

The Bible for little children, *by Maïte Roche*
(ISBN 1 86082 399 8 CTS Code CH 2)

The Gospel for little children, *by Maïte Roche*
(ISBN 1 86082 400 5 CTS Code CH 1)

The Rosary, *by Juliette Levivier*
(ISBN 1 86082 397 1 CTS Code CH 3)

The Way of the Cross, *by Juliette Levivier*
(ISBN 1 86082 398 X CTS Code CH 4)

First prayers for little children, *by Maïte Roche*
(ISBN 978 1 86082 443 2 CTS Code CH 5)

Praying with the friends of Jesus, *by Juliette Levivier*
(ISBN 978 1 86082 444 9 CTS Code CH 6)

Prayers around the Crib, *by Juliette Levivier*
(ISBN 978 1 86082 445 6 CTS Code CH 7)

The most beautiful Christmas Story, *by Maïte Roche*
(ISBN 978 1 86082 446 3 CTS Code CH 8)

Faith for children, *by Christine Pedotti*
(ISBN 978 1 86082 447 0 CTS Code CH 9)

Faith for children: Published 2007 by the Incorporated Catholic Truth Society, 40-46 Harleyford Road, London SE11 5AY. Tel: 020 7640 0042; Fax: 020 7640 0046; www.cts-online.org.uk. Copyright © 2007 The Incorporated Catholic Truth Society in this English-language edition.

ISBN: 978 1 86082 447 0   CTS Code CH 9

Le Livre de la foi des petits enfants pour préparer le catéchisme en famille by Christine Pedotti, illustrations by Éric Puybaret, published 2004 by Edifa-Mame, 15-27 rue Moussorgski, 75018 Paris; ISBN 2-7289-1105-3. Copyright © Groupe Fleurus 2004.